Dr. Abi Adeleke is a social media strategist and marketing strategies expert with over 10 years of experience helping businesses of all sizes grow their online presence.

Before earning a doctoral degree in Business Administration (Marketing Strategies specialization) at Walden University, Abi Adeleke worked with several leading companies in the Compliance arena.

Throughout Dr. Abi's career, she has helped several small businesses develop and implement effective social media strategies, increase brand awareness, and drive revenue growth. With a deep understanding of the ever-changing landscape of social media, Dr. Abi is passionate about empowering others to take control of their online presence and succeed in the digital age.

As an author, Dr. Abi has published several articles and blog posts on social media marketing, including the bestselling eBook "From Zero to Social Media Hero: Overcoming the Challenges of Starting on Social Media."

In this guide, Dr. Abi shares their proven tactics and strategies for building a strong social media presence from scratch, even if you need more followers.

Whether you're a small business owner looking to increase your online visibility or an aspiring social media influencer seeking to grow your following, "From Zero to Social Media Hero: Overcoming the Challenges of Starting on Social Media" is the ultimate guide to mastering the art of social media marketing.

Contents

Chapter 1: Introduction

Social media has revolutionized the way we connect and communicate with one another. It has become a powerful tool for businesses and individuals to engage with their audience, build brand awareness, and establish themselves as thought leaders in their respective industries. The importance of social media cannot be overstated, as it has become a vital aspect of modern life.

Social media provides businesses a platform to connect with customers on a deeper level. It allows them to showcase their products and services, share customer success stories, and communicate directly with their audience. Social media can help businesses build brand loyalty, increase customer engagement, and drive sales. In today's digital age, companies that fail to leverage the power of social media risk falling behind their competitors.

For individuals, social media provides a means of expressing themselves and connecting with like-minded individuals. It allows them to share their thoughts, ideas, and experiences with others and form meaningful connections with people worldwide. Social media can also be a source of inspiration, motivation, and support during challenging times. It can unite people and create community, even in adversity. Whether through sharing a personal story, a creative project, or a shared interest, social media can connect us all.

In conclusion, the importance of social media cannot be overstated. It has become an integral part of modern life, providing businesses and individuals with a platform to connect, engage, and communicate with others. From building brand awareness to fostering a sense of community, social media has the power to inspire, motivate, and empower us all. So, whether you're a business owner or an individual, it's time to embrace the power of social media and use it to your advantage.

Starting social media can be exciting, but it's not always a smooth ride. As with any new journey, there are challenges to be faced. For instance, when I started my first social media account, I had no idea what I was doing. I thought I could post pictures of my cat, and people would magically flock to my page. That didn't happen. Instead, I struggled to create content that people would want to see.

Another challenge that I faced was understanding the algorithms. As a beginner, I had no clue how social media algorithms worked. I would spend hours crafting the perfect post, only to have it buried in the feed within minutes. I quickly learned that understanding the algorithms is key to success on social media. It's all about timing, hashtags, and engagement.

Lastly, the sheer amount of competition can be overwhelming. When you start on social media, it can feel like you're shouting into a crowded room. Everyone else is vying for attention too, and it can be difficult to stand out from the noise. But, as with any new endeavor, perseverance and consistency pay off. With time and effort, I learned how to create content that resonated with my audience, and my following grew steadily.

Chapter 2: Identifying Goals and Audience

Welcome to Chapter 2: Identifying Goals and Audience. Before we dive into the serious stuff. It's about a time when I was asked to create a social media strategy for a local bakery. As I sat down with the owner to discuss their goals and target audience, I couldn't help but notice the delicious smell of freshly baked pastries wafting through the air.

Suddenly, my stomach rumbled so loudly that it interrupted our conversation. The owner looked at me with confusion and concern as I awkwardly explained that I hadn't had breakfast yet. We took a break to sample some of the bakery's delicious treats, and I realized: if identifying goals and audience is as delicious as these pastries, I might be in for a treat.

So, if you're ready to sink your teeth into some tasty insights about identifying goals and audiences for social media, let's get started!

Setting clear goals and objectives is essential for success on social media. Without a clear direction, your efforts can quickly become scattered and unfocused. Establishing goals and objectives helps you define what you want to achieve and leads you to success.

Here are six reasons why setting clear goals and objectives is crucial for social media success:

1. A clear direction: Goals and objectives provide a clear path for your social media efforts. They help you focus on what's important and stay on track toward achieving your desired outcomes.

2. Helps measure success: Clear goals and objectives allow you to measure your success and determine whether your social media efforts deliver the desired results. This enables you to identify

areas for improvement and make necessary adjustments.

3. Facilitates decision-making: When you have clear goals and objectives, it becomes easier to decide what content to post, which platforms to use, and how to engage with your audience. This helps you stay focused on your goals and avoid distractions.

4. Facilitates decision-making: When you have clear goals and objectives, it becomes easier to decide what content to post, which platforms to use, and how to engage with your audience. This helps you stay focused on your goals and avoid distractions.

5. Facilitates decision-making: When you have clear goals and objectives, it becomes easier to decide what content to post, which platforms to use, and how to engage with your audience. This helps you stay focused on your goals and avoid distractions.

6. Facilitates decision-making: When you have clear goals and objectives, it becomes easier to decide what content to post, which platforms to use, and how to engage with your audience. This helps you stay focused on your goals and avoid distractions.

Five action items to help you set clear goals and objectives for social media:

1. **Define your objectives**: What do you want to achieve through your social media efforts? Are you looking to increase brand awareness, drive traffic to your website, or generate leads? Defining your objectives will help you create a clear direction for your social media efforts.

2. **Identify your target audience:** Who are you trying to reach? What are their interests and pain points? Understanding your target audience will help you create content that resonates with them and drives engagement.

3. **Choose your platforms:** Which social media platforms are most relevant to

your target audience? Are you targeting a B2B audience, in which case LinkedIn might be your best platform? Or are you targeting a younger audience, in which case Instagram or TikTok might be more appropriate?

4. **Develop a content strategy:** Once you have identified your objectives and target audience and chosen your platforms, you must create a content strategy. Your content strategy should align with your objectives and be tailored to your target audience.

5. **Measure your success:** Regularly measure your success against your objectives. This will help you identify what's working and what's not and make necessary adjustments to your strategy.

In conclusion, setting clear goals and objectives is crucial for social media success. It provides a clear direction, helps measure success, facilitates decision-making, encourages collaboration, increases accountability, and helps allocate resources effectively. By following the above action items, you can set clear goals and objectives for your social media efforts and work towards achieving success.

Identifying and understanding your target audience

Identifying and understanding your target audience is critical in creating a successful social media strategy. Without a clear understanding of your audience, social media efforts can become unfocused and ineffective. Here are six key steps to identifying and understanding your target audience:

1. **Conduct research:** Researching your target audience is essential. You can use tools like Google Analytics, social media analytics, and customer surveys to gather information about your audience's demographics, interests, and behavior.

2. **Develop buyer personas:** Buyer personas are fictional representations of your ideal customers. They help you understand your target audience better by providing a clear picture of who they are, what they do, and what motivates them. Use templates or create your own to help you develop your buyer personas.

3. **Analyze competitors:** Analyzing your competitors can give you insights into their target audience and help you identify gaps in the market. Look at their social media profiles, website, and marketing campaigns to understand their target audience.

4. **Use social listening:** Social listening involves monitoring social media channels to understand what people say about your brand, competitors, and industry. This can help you identify trends and insights about your target audience that you might not have discovered otherwise.

5. **Conduct surveys and focus groups**: Surveys and focus groups can provide valuable insights into your target audience's preferences and behavior. Use a template or create your own to help you develop your survey questions and conduct your focus groups.

6. **Develop a workbook:** Use a workbook to gather all the information you have collected about your target audience in one place. Include your buyer personas, research findings, competitor analysis, social listening insights, survey and focus group results, and other relevant information.

To help you get started on identifying and understanding your target audience, here are some exercises and templates you can use:

Buyer persona template: Use a template to create your buyer personas. Include details like demographics, job titles, pain points, and motivations. You can find free templates online or create your own.

1. Personal Information

Name:

Age:

Gender:

Occupation:

Marital Status:

Education Level:

Income:

2. Demographics

Location:

Language:

Culture:

Family size:

Homeownership:

3. Psychographics

Interests:

Hobbies:

Personality traits:

Values:

Attitudes:

Lifestyle:

4. Behavior Shopping Habits

Online Habits:

Technology Use:

Media Consumption:

Buying Triggers:

Purchasing Objections:

5. **Goals and Challenges**

Primary Goal:

Secondary Goal:

Challenges Faced:

Pain Points:

Fears:

6. **Marketing Message**

Key Message:

Unique Selling Proposition:

Brand Perception:

Call to Action:

7. **Buyer Journey Awareness Stage:**

Consideration Stage:

Decision Stage:

Post-Purchase Stage:

You can use this template to create a detailed buyer persona that will help you understand your target audience better and tailor your marketing strategies accordingly.

Remember to be specific and base your information on research and data.

Social media analytics template: Use a template to track your analytics. Include metrics like engagement rate, reach, and impressions. This will help you understand which content resonates with your audience and where you need to improve.

Overview Date Range:

- Total Impressions:
- Total Reach:
- Engagement Rate:
- Follower Growth:
- Top Performing Posts:
- Top Performing Hashtags:
- Top Performing Content Types:
- Platform Specific Metrics

Facebook:

- Page Likes:
- Post Likes:
- Comments:
- Shares:

Instagram:

- Followers:
- Likes:
- Comments:
- Saves:

Twitter:

- Followers:
- Retweets:
- Likes:
- Replies:

LinkedIn:

- Followers:
- Impressions:
- Clicks:
- Engagement:

Audience Insights Demographics:

- Age:
- Gender:
- Location:
- Interests:

- Topics:

Hashtags:

- Brands:
- Behavior:
- Active Times:
- Devices:
- Source of Traffic:

Campaign Performance:

- Campaign Name:
- Goal:
- Impressions:
- Reach:
- Clicks:
- Conversion Rate:
- Cost per Click:
- Return on Investment:
- Competitor Analysis
- Competitor Name:
- Follower Count:
- Engagement Rate:
- Top Performing Posts:
- Top Performing Hashtags:
- Key Insights:

Competitor analysis template: Use a template to conduct a competitor analysis. Include information like their target audience, messaging, and marketing campaigns. This will help you identify gaps in the market and opportunities for differentiation.

1. Competitor Information •

Competitor Name:

- Industry:

- Products/Services Offered:

- Target Market:

- Unique Selling Proposition:

2. Website Analysis

- Website Traffic:

- Website Design/Navigation:

- User Experience:

- Search Engine Ranking:

- Content Quality:

- Calls to Action:

- Lead Generation Strategies:

3. Social Media Analysis

- Social Media Platforms Used:

- Follower Count:

- Engagement Rate:

- Content Strategy:

- Advertising Strategies:

- Audience Insights:

- Influencer Partnerships:

4. Marketing Strategies

- Advertising Channels Used:

- Promotions and Discounts Offered:

• Email Marketing:

• Content Marketing:

• Events and Sponsorships: • Public Relations:

5. Strengths and Weaknesses

• Competitor Strengths: • Competitor Weaknesses: • Opportunities for Your Business: • Threats to Your Business:

6. Conclusion • Key Takeaways: • Action Plan: • Next Steps:

Use this template to thoroughly analyze your competitors to gain insights into their strategies and identify areas where your business can improve. Remember to regularly review and update your analysis to stay informed about changes in the market and your competitors' strategies.

Survey and focus group questions template: Use a template to develop your survey and guide group questions. Make sure your questions are open-ended and provide you with actionable insights.

Survey Questions:

1. Demographic Information

- What is your age?

- What is your gender?

- What is your occupation?

- What is your income level?

- What is your educational background?

- What is your marital status?

- What is your location?

2. Product/Service Usage

- Have you ever used our product/service?

- How often do you use our product/service?

- What do you like/dislike about our product/service?

- How satisfied are you with our product/service?

- What factors influence your decision to use our product/service?

- Have you recommended our product/service to others?

3. Customer Service

- How was your experience with our customer service?

- Was your issue resolved to your satisfaction?

- Did you find our customer service representatives helpful and knowledgeable?

- How can we improve our customer service?

4. Brand Perception

• How familiar are you with our brand?

• What do you think of our brand?

• How does our brand compare to competitors?

• What are the strengths and weaknesses of our brand?

• What can we do to improve our brand image?

Focus Group Questions

1. Introduction

• Can you introduce yourself and tell us a little about your background?

• Have you ever used our product/service before?

• What was your experience with our product/service like?

2. Product/Service Discussion

• What do you like/dislike about our product/service?

• What are the most important factors to you when using our product/service?

• How does our product/service compare to competitors?

• What changes or improvements would you suggest for our product/service?

3. Customer Service Discussion

• Have you had any experiences with our customer service?

• How was your experience with our customer service?

• What could we do to improve our customer service?

4. Brand Perception Discussion

• What comes to mind when you think of our brand?

• How does our brand compare to competitors?

• What do you think are the strengths and weaknesses of our brand?

• How can we improve our brand image?

Use this template to gather customer insights and improve your product/service and brand image. Remember to ask open-ended questions to encourage discussion and use the responses to guide your decision-making.

Workbook template: Use a template to create your workbook. Include all the information you have gathered about your target audience in one place. This will help you stay organized and focused as you develop your social media strategy.

1. Introduction • Purpose of the Workbook:

• Target Audience:

• Instructions on How to Use the Workbook:

• Disclaimer:

2. Goals and Objectives

• Define the Goals and Objectives:

• Break Down the Goals and Objectives into Smaller Tasks:

• Assign Tasks to Team Members:

3. Timeline

• Define the Timeline:

• Assign Deadlines to Tasks:

• Create a Visual Timeline (Gantt Chart, Calendar, etc.):

4. Resources

• List the Required Resources:

• Assign Responsibilities for Acquiring Resources:

• Set Budgets for Each Resource:

5. Metrics

Define the Metrics to Measure Success:

• Establish Baseline Metrics:

• Monitor and Report Progress Regularly:

6. Challenges and Risks

• Identify Potential Challenges and Risks:

• Determine the Likelihood and Impact of Each Risk:

• Create a Contingency Plan for Each Risk:

7. Conclusion

• Recap the Goals and Objectives:

• Recap the Timeline:

• Recap the Resources:

• Recap the Metrics:

• Recap the Challenges and Risks:

• Action Plan for Next Steps:
Use this template to create a comprehensive workbook for your project or initiative. Remember to regularly update the workbook as progress is made and circumstances change.

In conclusion, identifying and understanding your target audience is essential for creating a successful social media strategy. You can gain valuable insights into your audience's preferences and behavior by researching, developing buyer personas, analyzing competitors, using social listening, conducting surveys and focus groups, and creating a workbook. Use the templates and exercises provided to help you get started on your target audience research.

Case studies and examples of effective goal setting and audience identification

Case Study 1: The Lip-Syncing Accountant

Bob was a strait-laced accountant who wanted to promote his business on social media. He knew he needed to identify his target audience and set clear goals to succeed. After some research, he discovered that his target audience was millennials interested in finance but found it boring.

Bob created a lip-syncing video series where he would lip-sync to popular songs while incorporating finance tips and advice. He set a goal of gaining 1,000 followers in six months. To his surprise, his videos went viral, and he gained 10,000 followers in just two months.

- Identifying your target audience can help you create content that resonates with them.
- Setting clear goals helps you stay focused and motivated.
- Don't be afraid to try something different and unexpected.

Case Study 2: The Coffee Shop Owner

Sarah owned a small coffee shop in a crowded city. She wanted to increase foot traffic and sales but wasn't sure how to reach her target audience. After researching, she discovered that her target audience was young professionals interested in specialty coffee and loved cute and aesthetic Instagram posts.

Sarah decided to create a unique Instagram account where she would post pictures of her cute coffee shop and showcase her specialty coffee. She set a goal of gaining 500 followers in six months. Within two months, she had gained over 1,000 followers, and her shop had become a go-to spot for young professionals.

- Knowing your target audience's interests and preferences can help you create content that appeals to them.
- Setting a realistic goal can help you measure your success.
- Consistency is key when it comes to social media.

Case Study 3: The Dentist

Dr. Smith was a dentist who wanted to increase his patient base. He knew his target audience was people who feared the dentist and needed to overcome their fear. He set a goal of improving patient appointments by 20% within six months.

Dr. Smith created a social media campaign to showcase his gentle and pain-free dentistry techniques. He also offered a free consultation to new patients who scheduled an appointment through social media. Within four months, he exceeded his goal and increased his patient appointments by 25%.

- Understanding your target audience's pain points can help you create a campaign that meets their needs.
- Offering incentives and promotions can help motivate people to act.
- Tracking your progress and adjusting your strategy can help you achieve your goals.

In conclusion, setting clear goals and identifying your target audience can lead to social media success. These case studies show that you can create content that resonates with them and achieve your goals by understanding your audience's interests, preferences, and pain points. Remember to be creative, consistent, and willing to try new things.

Chapter 3: Choosing the Right Platform

Are you tired of feeling like a lonely soul lost in the vast sea of social media platforms? Are you scrolling aimlessly through Instagram, Twitter, Facebook, and LinkedIn, unsure where to focus your efforts? Well, fear not, my friend, for you have stumbled upon the chapter that will guide you through the treacherous waters of choosing the right platform.

Think of it as a game of 'The Bachelor,' but instead of choosing a significant other, you choose the perfect social media platform to fall in love with. Each forum is like a contestant vying for your attention, trying to woo you with its unique features and user base. Will you fall for the charming and aesthetically pleasing Instagram? Or will you choose the witty and engaging Twitter? The choice is yours, my friend, and we're here to help you make it.

So, sit back, grab some popcorn, and get ready for the social media version of 'The Bachelor.' And who knows, maybe you'll even find your perfect match.

The different types of social media platforms and their respective strengths and weaknesses.

Social media has revolutionized the way we communicate and connect with others. With so many platforms, knowing which ones to use for your business or personal brand can be overwhelming. To help you navigate the world of social media, we've broken down the different types of platforms and their respective strengths and weaknesses.

Social Networking Sites: These platforms focus on building individual connections and relationships. Facebook is the most popular social networking site, with over 2 billion active users worldwide. It's great for staying in touch with friends and family, joining groups with shared interests, and creating a business page to connect with customers.

Microblogging Sites: These platforms allow users to post short real-time updates, such as text or images. Twitter is the most well-known microblogging site, with over 330 million active users. It's great for engaging with customers, sharing news and updates, and participating in trending topics.

Visual Sharing Sites: These platforms share visual content, such as photos and videos. Instagram is the most popular visual-sharing site, with over 1 billion active users. It's great for showcasing products, creating visually appealing content, and reaching a younger demographic.

Professional Networking Sites: These platforms focus on building professional connections and promoting career growth. LinkedIn is the most popular professional networking site, with over 700 million active users. It's great for networking with other professionals, sharing industry-related news and updates, and promoting your brand.

Video Sharing Sites: These platforms focus on sharing video content. YouTube is the most popular video-sharing site, with over 2 billion active users. It's great for creating educational content, showcasing products, and reaching a large audience.

Discussion Forums: These platforms allow users to create and participate in online discussions around specific topics. Reddit is the most popular discussion forum, with over 430 million active users. It's great for connecting with like-minded individuals, gathering feedback, and sharing knowledge and expertise.

It's important to note that each platform has strengths and weaknesses; the best one for you will depend on your goals and target audience. By understanding the different types of social media platforms and their respective strengths and weaknesses, you can decide which ones to use for your business or personal brand.

How to choose the right platform based on your goals and audience.

Choosing the right social media platform is crucial for the success of your business or personal brand. It's not enough to be on social media - you need to be on the right platforms to help you reach your goals and target audience. But with so many options, how do you know which ones are right for you? Fear not, my friend, for we have the ultimate guide on choosing the right platform based on your goals and audience.

1. **Define your goals**: Before choosing a platform, it's important to define them. Are you looking to increase brand awareness, drive sales, or engage with customers? Each forum has its strengths and weaknesses, so choosing one that aligns with your goals is important.

2. **Know your audience:** Understanding your target audience is key to choosing the right platform. Are they younger or older, male, or female, tech-savvy or not? Knowing their demographics and interests will help you pick a platform they're already using and will be most receptive to.

3. **Know your audience**: Understanding your target audience is key to choosing the right platform. Are they younger or older, male, or female, tech-savvy or not? Knowing their demographics and interests will help you pick a platform

they're already using and will be most receptive to.

4. **Evaluate platform features:** Each platform has unique features, such as Instagram's visually appealing grid and Twitter's real-time updates. Evaluate these features and how they align with your goals and audience. For example, if you want to showcase products, Instagram's visual focus may be the best option.

5. **Consider your resources:** It's important to consider your available resources, such as time and budget when choosing a platform. If you don't have the resources to create consistent, high-quality video content, then YouTube may not be your best option.

6. **Test and adjust:** Finally, don't be afraid to test different platforms and adapt your strategy as needed. Finding the right platform for your goals and audience may take some trial and error,

but by testing and adjusting, you can ultimately find success.

By following these steps, you'll be well on your way to choosing the right social media platform for your business or personal brand. Remember to stay true to your goals and audience, and don't be afraid to try new things. With the right platform and strategy, you can achieve social media success and reach your desired audience.

10 Tips for Optimizing Your Presence on Social Media Platforms:

1. **Consistency is key:** Post regularly and at optimal times for your audience.
2. **Use engaging visuals:** Images and videos perform better than text-only posts.
3. **Keep your branding consistent:** Use the same profile picture, cover photo, and color scheme across all platforms.
4. **Be human and personable:** social media is about connecting with others,

so don't be afraid to show your personality.

5. **Use hashtags:** They can help your posts reach a wider audience and increase discoverability.

6. **Engage with your followers:** Respond to comments and messages promptly to build relationships.

7. **Share user-generated content:** It's a great way to show appreciation for your followers and create a sense of community.

8. **Utilize analytics:** Use platform-specific analytics to track your performance and adjust your strategy accordingly.

9. **Experiment with different types of content:** Try out other formats, such as live videos or polls, to keep your audience engaged.

10. **Stay updated with platform updates:** Social media platforms constantly evolve, so keep up with new features and changes.

10 Action Items for Optimizing Your Presence on Social Media Platforms:

1. Create a content calendar and schedule posts in advance.

2. Take high-quality photos or create engaging graphics to accompany your posts.

3. Use a tool like Canva to create branded social media graphics.

4. Write a brand bio that communicates who you are and what you do.

5. Respond to comments and messages within 24 hours.

6. Set aside time each week to interact with other accounts in your niche.

7. Encourage followers to share their experiences with your brand using a branded hashtag.

8. Use platform-specific analytics tools like Facebook Insights or Twitter Analytics to track your performance.

9. Try out a new type of content, such as Instagram Reels or Twitter Spaces.

10. Read the latest platform updates and experiment with new features to stay ahead of the curve.

By implementing these tips and acting on these items, you can optimize your presence on social media platforms and increase your engagement and reach. Remember to stay true to your brand and audience, and always be willing to try new things and adjust your strategy accordingly.

Chapter 4: Content Creation and Curation

It's time to get creative and let those social media juices flow! Or, if you're like me, it's time to stare at a blank screen for hours, wondering why your brain suddenly turned into a bowl of oatmeal.

Welcome to Chapter 4: Content Creation and Curation. This is where the magic happens, or you have a mental breakdown and start questioning your life choices. Don't worry; we've all been there.

Creating and curating content can be both exciting and daunting. With so much competition, standing out and capturing your audience's attention can be hard. But fear not, my friends! With the right tools and strategies, you can create content that engages your audience and showcases your brand's unique personality.

So, let's roll up our sleeves, put on our thinking caps, and dive into the wonderful world of content creation and curation. Or we can stare at funny cat videos for a few hours. No judgment here.

The importance of creating and sharing high-quality, relevant content.

Strategies for creating effective social media content.

Social media is about creating content that captivates your audience and makes them want to engage with your brand. But how do you create content that stands out in a sea of noise? This section will explore strategies for creating effective social media content that will help you connect with your audience and achieve your goals.

1. **Know your audience:** The first step to creating effective social media content is understanding your audience. What are their interests, pain points, and motivations? Use this information to create content that resonates with them.

2. **Tell a story:** People love stories, so incorporate storytelling into social media content. Use personal anecdotes, customer testimonials, or case studies to make your content more relatable.

3. **Be visual:** Visual content is more engaging than text, so include images, videos, and infographics in your social media posts. Use high-quality visuals that are relevant to your content.
4. **Use humor:** Humor is a great way to connect with your audience and make them feel good. Just make sure your humor is appropriate for your brand and audience.
5. **Be authentic:** Authenticity is key to building trust with your audience. Be true to your brand's voice and values, and don't try to be something you're not.

Additional strategies for creating effective social media content:

1. **Provide value:** Give your audience something they can use or learn from. Create how-to guides, tutorials, or industry news updates.
2. **Use user-generated content:** User-generated content is a great way to showcase your brand's personality and build trust with your audience. Share

customer photos, testimonials, or reviews.

3. **Be timely**: Create content that is timely and relevant to your audience. This could include holiday-themed content or content that ties into current events.

4. **Repurpose content**: Don't reinvent the wheel every time you create content—Repurpose content from your blog, website, or other social media channels to save time and effort.

5. **Experiment:** Don't be afraid to try new things with your content. Experiment with different formats, topics, and strategies to see what works best for your brand.

Action items:

1. Conduct audience research to understand your target audience.

2. Develop a content calendar to plan out your social media content in advance.

3. Use different visual content, including images, videos, and infographics.

4. Experiment with humor and storytelling to make your content more engaging.

5. Repurpose content from other channels to save time and effort.

Curating content from other sources can be a great way to supplement your content and provide value to your audience. Here are ten simple but engaging techniques for curating content from other sources:

1. **Follow industry influencers:** Keep up to date with the latest news and trends in your industry by following influencers on social media platforms.

2. **Set up Google Alerts:** Set up alerts for keywords related to your industry to receive notifications when new content is published.

3. **Use RSS feeds**: Subscribe to RSS feeds for relevant blogs and websites to easily access their latest content.

4. **Share relevant content from other social media accounts:** Share content

from other social media accounts relevant to your audience.

5. **Use social bookmarking sites:** Bookmark and tag relevant content on social bookmarking sites like Reddit, Pocket, or Mix to access it later easily.

6. **Curate lists:** Create lists of top industry blogs, websites, or thought leaders to share with your audience.

7. **Collaborate with other businesses:** Collaborate with other companies or influencers in your industry to co-create content or share each other's content.

8. Use content discovery tools like Feedly, BuzzSumo, or ContentGems to discover and curate relevant content.

9. **Share user-generated content**: Share content created by your audience, such as customer reviews or user-generated photos.

10. **Repurpose content**: Repurpose content from other sources into a different format,

such as turning a blog post into an infographic or video.

Using these techniques, you can easily curate content from other sources and provide value to your audience. Just give credit where credit is due and follow proper citation and linking practices.

Tools and resources for content creation and curation. *Here is an outline of simple tools and resources for content creation and curation:*

Content Creation Tools

A. Graphic Design

- Canva
- Adobe Spark
- Piktochart

B. Video Creation and Editing

- Animoto
- Filmora
- iMovie (for Mac users)

C. Writing and Editing

- Grammarly
- Hemingway Editor
- Google Docs

Content Curation Tools

A. Content Discovery

- Feedly
- BuzzSumo
- ContentGems

B. Social Media Management

- Hootsuite
- Buffer
- Sprout Social

C. Bookmarking and Tagging

- Pockct
- Mix
- Evernote

D. Additional Resources

Additional Resources

A. Stock Photos and Videos

- Unsplash
- Pexels
- Shutterstock

B. Content Planning and Organization

- Trello

- Asana
- CoSchedule

C. Analytics and Insights

- Google Analytics
- Facebook Insights
- Twitter Analytics

These tools and resources can help make content creation and curation easier and more efficient. It's important to find the best tools for you and your specific needs and to continually assess and adjust your strategy to ensure the best results.

Chapter 5: Building A Community

Are you ready to build a tighter community than your skinny jeans after Thanksgiving dinner? Then buckle up, buttercup, because we're diving into Chapter 5: Building a community.

But first, let me tell you a story. Once upon a time, a social media manager thought building a community was as easy as throwing a few hashtags on a post and calling it a day. Boy, was she wrong? She quickly realized that building a community takes hard work, dedication, and some magic.

So, if you're feeling overwhelmed by the thought of creating a community, don't worry. We've got you covered with some tips and tricks to make your followers feel like part of the family. Let's get started!

The value of building a community on social media

Building a community on social media is not just about gaining more followers and likes. It's about creating a loyal group of individuals who believe in your brand and are invested in what you have to offer. Here are some key reasons why building a community is essential for your social media strategy:

1. **Increased brand awareness:** By building a community, you can reach a wider audience and increase brand awareness. Your followers will be more likely to share your content with their followers, leading to a greater reach and potential new customers.

2. **Stronger customer relationships:** Building a community allows you to connect with your customers more personally. This can lead to stronger relationships and increased customer loyalty.

3. **Improved customer service:** When you build a community, you create a space where customers can ask questions and provide feedback. Engaging with your followers can offer better customer service and improve your overall business operations.

4. **Increased sales:** A strong community can increase sales as your followers are more likely to buy from a brand they trust and feel connected with.

5. **Valuable insights:** Your community can provide valuable insights into your target audience, allowing you to tailor your content and messaging to better suit their needs.

Some key takeaways to consider when building a community on social media:

1. **Focus on engagement:** Building a community requires active attention from your followers. Respond to comments and messages promptly and encourage conversation among your followers.

2. **Provide value:** Your content should provide value to your followers, whether it's through informative blog posts, entertaining videos, or engaging social media posts.

3. **Consistency is key:** Consistency is important when building a community. Post regularly and simultaneously weekly to create a sense of reliability and dependability.
4. **Listen to your audience:** Pay attention to what your followers say and adjust your content and strategy accordingly.
5. **Be authentic:** Building a community requires authenticity and transparency. Be true to your brand, and your followers will appreciate it.

Building a community on social media takes time and effort, but the rewards are worth it. By focusing on engagement, providing value, and being authentic, you can create a community invested in your brand and eager to support your business.

Strategies for engaging with your audience and building relationships.
1. **Respond promptly**: The quicker you respond, the better. People expect a timely response, and a quick reply can defuse a situation before it escalates.

2. **Be empathetic:** Try understanding the commenter's perspective and putting yourself in their shoes. This can help you respond in a more understanding and supportive way.

3. **Stay calm:** It's easy to get defensive when someone leaves negative comments or criticism, but it's important to stay calm and composed when responding. Take a few deep breaths before crafting your response.

4. **Address the issue:** Make sure to address the commenter's concern directly. Whether it's a complaint or a question, respond thoughtfully to their specific problem.

5. **Be courteous:** Always be polite and professional when responding to comments, even if the comment is negative. Remember, your response reflects your brand, so represent it well.

6. **Personalize your response:** Whenever possible, personalize your answer to the

commenter. Address them by name and acknowledge their specific concern.

7. **Provide a solution:** If the commenter has a problem or issue, provide a solution or next steps to help resolve the situation.

8. **Invite further discussion:** Encourage further discussion and engagement by asking open-ended questions and inviting the commenter to share their thoughts or ideas.

9. **Say thank you:** Always thank the commenter for taking the time to leave a comment or provide feedback, even if it's negative.

10. **Monitor and follow up:** After responding to a comment, monitor the conversation and follow up if necessary. This shows that you care about your audience and value their input.

Best practices for responding to comments, feedback, and criticism.

1. **Respond promptly:** Respond to comments and feedback as soon as possible. This shows that you value your followers' input and are engaged with your audience.

2. **Stay professional:** No matter how negative or harsh the comment or feedback may be, always respond professionally and respectfully. Avoid getting defensive or aggressive.

3. **Address the issue directly:** If someone is providing feedback or criticism about a specific topic, address that issue directly and respond thoughtfully. This shows that you take their feedback seriously and are willing to improve.

4. **Show appreciation:** Thank followers for their positive feedback and comments. This encourages them to continue engaging with your brand.

5. **Be transparent:** If you made a mistake, apologize for it. Honesty and

transparency go a long way in building trust with your audience.

6. **Keep it concise:** Keep your responses brief and to the point. Avoid going off on tangents or getting too wordy.

7. **Use humor if appropriate:** Feel free to use humor if the comment or feedback lends itself to humor. Humor can be a great way to defuse a tense situation.

8. **Take conversations offline if necessary:** If the issue requires a more detailed discussion or resolution, take it offline. Provide the person with an email address or phone number where they can contact you directly.

9. **Don't engage with trolls:** If someone leaves negative comments or feedback to be disruptive or hurtful, don't engage with them. It's okay to delete their comments or block them from your page.

10. **Learn from the feedback:** Use feedback and criticism as an opportunity to learn and grow. Take constructive

criticism to heart and use it to improve your brand and social media presence.

Case studies and examples of successful community building on social media.

Case Study #1: **Purrfect Community Building** A local animal shelter started a social media campaign to build a community of pet lovers. They posted funny and heartwarming pictures and videos of the animals in their care and encouraged their followers to share their pet stories. They also hosted a weekly Q&A session with their shelter veterinarian to answer pet-related questions. Within a few months, their social media following had skyrocketed, and they could find homes for more animals than ever before.

Key Takeaways:

Know your audience: The shelter knew its target audience was pet lovers, and they created content that would appeal to them.

Engagement is key: Encouraging followers to share their stories and ask questions creates a sense of community and engagement.

Have a clear goal: The shelter's goal was to find homes for animals, and their social media campaign directly helped them achieve that.

Case Study #2: Community Building with a Side of Sarcasm A fast food chain humorously approached its social media strategy. They created a snarky, tongue-in-cheek persona that was unapologetically irreverent. They engaged with their followers through witty comments and memes and even made viral videos poking fun at themselves. The result? A massive following of fans who loved their brand's sense of humor.

Key Takeaways:

Be authentic: The fast-food chain knew its brand persona and stayed true to it, even if it meant being irreverent.

Humor can be a powerful tool: A sense of humor can effectively connect with your audience and build a community of engaged followers.

Take risks: The chain was willing to take risks and push boundaries, which helped set them apart from other fast-food brands.

Case Study #3: Community Building Through Education A beauty brand created a social media campaign to educate its followers about skin care. They posted videos featuring dermatologists answering common skin care questions and sharing tips and tricks. They also created infographics and blog posts about skincare myths and best practices. Their campaign helped educate their followers and built a community of engaged beauty enthusiasts.

Key Takeaways:
Provide value: The beauty brand provided valuable information and education to their followers, which helped establish them as experts in their field.
Use various content types: The brand used videos, infographics, and blog posts to appeal to different learners.

Align with your brand values: The brand's commitment to education and transparency in skincare aligned with its overall brand values.

Chapter 6: Measuring Success and ROI

Welcome to Chapter 6, where we'll discuss measuring success and ROI on social media. I know what you're thinking: "Oh great, another chapter about boring numbers and analytics. Can't we skip to the cat memes?" But trust me, this chapter will be more fun than a barrel of monkeys on Twitter.

We all know that social media can be a time-sucking black hole, and getting lost in the endless scroll of likes, comments, and shares is easy. But if you invest your time and resources into building a social media presence, you must know whether it's making a difference. That's where measuring success and ROI come in. And don't worry; we won't be drowning in spreadsheets and graphs. We'll make it as painless as possible; I promise.

So put down the cat videos (just for a minute, I promise they'll still be there when we're done), and let's dive into the world of measuring success and ROI on social media.

Understanding social media metrics and analytics

Understanding social media metrics and analytics is a crucial aspect of measuring the success of your social media strategy. Metrics provide insights into how your audience engages with your content and can help you identify areas for improvement. With the vast amount of data available, it can be overwhelming to know where to start.

First and foremost, it's important to determine which metrics are most relevant to your goals. For example, metrics such as reach, and impressions are important if your goal is to increase brand awareness. If your goal is to drive website traffic, click-through rates and referral traffic are more relevant. Understanding your goals and what you want to achieve is crucial in selecting the right metrics to measure.

Once you've identified which metrics to measure, it's important to use the right tools to track them. Many social media platforms, such as Facebook Insights and Twitter Analytics, provide built-in analytics. These tools allow you to track metrics such as engagement, reach, and follower demographics. There are also third-party tools available that provide more in-depth analysis and reporting.

When analyzing your metrics, it's important to look beyond surface-level numbers. For example, high engagement rates are great, but it's important to analyze what type of engagement you're receiving. Are your followers leaving meaningful comments and sharing your content, or are they simply liking your posts? Understanding engagement quality can help you tailor your content to resonate better with your audience.

Tracking metrics over time is also important for identifying trends and patterns. Monitoring your metrics regularly lets you see your strategy's performance and adjust as needed. This can help you optimize your social media strategy to achieve your goals.

Finally, it's important to remember that metrics are only one part of the story. While they provide valuable insights into your content's performance, they don't tell the full story of your brand's impact on social media. It's also important to consider qualitative factors, such as brand sentiment and overall perception.

In summary, understanding social media metrics and analytics is a crucial aspect of measuring the success of your social media strategy. By selecting the right metrics to measure, using the right tools to track them, analyzing beyond surface-level numbers, tracking metrics over time, and considering qualitative factors, you can gain valuable insights into how your brand performs on social media and optimize your strategy accordingly.

Setting benchmarks and tracking progress toward your goals

Setting standards and monitoring progress towards your goals is crucial for measuring success and ROI on social media. It's easy to get caught up in the numbers and lose sight of what you're trying to achieve, but setting clear benchmarks can help you stay focused and on track.

The first step is to identify and break your goals into measurable metrics. For example, you might track metrics such as reach, impressions, and engagement to increase brand awareness. If you desire to generate leads, you might track metrics such as website clicks, form submissions, and conversions.

Once you have your benchmarks in place, tracking them consistently over time is important. This will allow you to see trends and identify areas to adjust. Various tools are available to help you track your metrics, including social media analytics platforms, website analytics tools, and even simple spreadsheets.

One key takeaway when tracking progress is not getting too caught up in vanity metrics. Just because you have many followers or likes doesn't necessarily mean you're achieving your goals. It's important to focus on metrics that are directly tied to your business objectives.

Another important consideration is to be patient. Building a social media presence takes time, and it's unlikely that you'll see results overnight. Staying committed and consistent and adjusting based on your progress is important.

Finally, it's important to celebrate your successes along the way. When you hit a milestone or achieve a goal, take a moment to recognize your accomplishments and reward yourself and your team. This will help keep you motivated and energized as you track progress toward your goals.

Calculating and evaluating the ROI of your social media efforts

Determine your goals: To calculate ROI, you first need to determine your social media goals, such as increasing brand awareness, generating leads, or driving sales.

Assign values to your goals: Assign values to your goals so you can track progress towards achieving them. For example, you can assign a value of $10 per lead generated from social media.

Track metrics: Use social media analytics tools to track metrics such as reach, engagement, website traffic, and conversions.

Monitor your social media spend: Track how much you spend on advertising, content creation, and community management.

Use a tracking URL: Use tracking URLs to measure the effectiveness of your social media campaigns and track the traffic they generate.

Calculate your social media costs: Add up all your costs, including advertising spend, content creation, and community management.

Calculate your social media revenue: Calculate the revenue generated by your social media efforts, such as sales generated through social media campaigns or leads that convert into paying customers.

Calculate your social media ROI: To calculate your ROI, divide your social media revenue by your social media posts, then multiply the result by 100 to get a percentage.

Monitor and adjust your social media efforts and adjust your strategy as needed to improve ROI.

Compare with industry benchmarks: Compare your social media ROI with industry benchmarks to see how you are performing compared to competitors in your industry.

Remember, calculating ROI for social media can be complex and may require the help of a marketing professional. However, following these tips can help you better understand the effectiveness of your social media efforts and make data-driven decisions to improve your ROI.

Tools and resources for measuring success and ROI.

Social Media Analytics Tools - Several free and paid tools are available that help track and analyze social media metrics, such as engagement rates, follower growth, and website traffic. Some popular tools include

Google Analytics, Hootsuite Insights, and Sprout Social.

Tracking URLs - Tracking URLs is a simple and effective way to measure the success of social media campaigns. These unique URLs allow you to track the traffic from each social media platform and see how many clicks and conversions you're getting.

Hashtag Analytics - Hashtags are a powerful tool for increasing reach and engagement on social media, and tracking their performance is essential. Tools like Hashtagify and RiteTag help you find relevant hashtags and measure their effectiveness.

A/B Testing - A/B testing involves creating two versions of a post or ad and testing them to see which performs better. This method can help you optimize your content for maximum engagement and ROI.

Social Listening Tools - Social listening tools like Mention and Brandwatch allow you to monitor social media for mentions of your brand, competitors, or industry keywords. This can help you understand customer sentiment, identify opportunities for engagement, and track the success of your social media campaigns.

Google Analytics - Google Analytics is a powerful tool for measuring website traffic and conversions from social media. By setting up goals and tracking URLs, you can see how much traffic and revenue your social media efforts generate.

Key takeaways:

- Use free and paid tools to track and analyze social media metrics.
- Tracking URLs, hashtag analytics, and A/B testing are effective ways to measure the success of social media campaigns.
- Social listening tools allow you to monitor brand mentions and customer sentiment on social media.
- Google Analytics is a powerful tool for measuring website traffic and conversions from social media.

Chapter 7: Overcoming Challenges and Obstacles

Are you ready for some real talk? Let's face it, building a successful social media presence isn't always a walk in the park. It's more like trying to navigate a minefield blindfolded. When you think you've got the hang of it, a new challenge throws you off balance. But fear not, my friend. This chapter is all about tackling those challenges head-on and emerging victorious on the other side.

Think of it like playing a video game, where each level presents new obstacles to overcome. Instead of jumping over barrels and dodging fireballs, you'll deal with trolls, algorithm changes, and creative burnout. At least you don't have to worry about losing any lives.

So, grab your power-ups, strap on your armor, and let's dive into the world of social media challenges.

Common challenges faced by businesses and individuals on social media.

Social media can be challenging, and businesses and individuals alike can face various obstacles when trying to make the most of their presence on these platforms. One common challenge is the ever-changing algorithms and trends that can make it difficult to keep up with what's popular and what's not. This can be especially frustrating for those who put a lot of time and effort into creating content only to find that it's not getting the engagement they had hoped for.

Another challenge is the potential for negative feedback and criticism. Social media gives everyone a voice; unfortunately, some people will use it to air their grievances and complaints. It's important to plan to respond to negative feedback constructively rather than getting defensive or lashing out.

Building a following and gaining traction on social media can also be a challenge, especially for those just starting. It can take time and effort to establish a presence and grow your audience, and it can be discouraging when progress is slow.

Another common challenge is keeping up with the demand for new content. Social media moves quickly, and users always look for something new and interesting to engage with. This can pressure businesses and individuals to constantly create new content, which can be difficult to sustain over time.

Finally, there's the challenge of staying authentic while still appealing to a wider audience. It can be tempting to try to appeal to the masses by conforming to popular trends and styles, but staying true to your voice and values is important.

To overcome these challenges, it's important to have a clear strategy in place for your social media presence. This should include setting realistic goals and benchmarks, identifying your target audience, and creating content that speaks to their interests and needs. It's also important to stay current on the latest trends and changes in the social media landscape and to be prepared to adapt your strategy as needed.

Key takeaways:

1. Social media can present various challenges, including changing algorithms, negative feedback, slow growth, and the demand for new content.

2. Having a clear strategy in place is important, including goals, benchmarks, and a target audience.

3. Responding to negative feedback constructively is key to maintaining a positive presence on social media.

4. Staying true to your voice and values is important for building a faithful following.

5. Keeping up with the latest trends and changes in the social media landscape is crucial for success.

6. Being prepared to adapt your strategy as needed can help you overcome obstacles and achieve your goals.

Strategies for overcoming challenges and obstacles include negative feedback, low engagement, and social media burnout.

1. Respond promptly and respectfully to negative feedback: Address negative feedback promptly and professionally. Show that you care about your audience's concerns and take their input seriously.

2. Use visuals and multimedia to increase engagement: Incorporate visuals, such as images and videos, into your content strategy to grab your audience's attention and increase engagement.

3. Experiment with different types of content: Try different types of content, such as user-generated content, polls,

and quizzes, to keep your audience interested and engaged.

4. Collaborate with other brands and influencers: Collaborating with different brands and influencers can help increase your reach and exposure to a wider audience.

5. Be consistent with your posting schedule: Set a consistent posting schedule to keep your audience engaged and interested in your content.

6. Engage with your audience: Show them you care about them by responding to comments, asking for feedback, and initiating conversations.

7. Take breaks and practice self-care: Social media burnout is real, so make sure to take breaks and practice self-

care to avoid getting overwhelmed and burnt out.

8. Monitor your analytics and adjust your strategy accordingly: Keep track of your social media analytics to see what's working and what's not. Use this data to adapt your strategy and optimize your content for better results.

9. Don't be afraid to try something new: Don't be scared to try new strategies and experiment with new ideas. Failure is okay, but you'll never know what works best for your audience if you don't try.

10. Stay authentic to your brand: Above all, stay faithful and true to your brand. Your audience will appreciate

your honesty and authenticity, which will help build trust and loyalty.

Case studies and examples of businesses and individuals who overcame challenges on social media.

The Donut Shop: **A small donut shop struggled to gain social media traction. They had very few followers, and their engagement rates were low. But then they came up with a genius idea: they started creating custom donuts based on popular memes and viral trends. Their followers loved it and soon got thousands of likes and shares on each post.**

Key takeaway: Don't be afraid to have fun and get creative with your content.

The Author: **An author was getting negative reviews on their latest book on social media. Rather than ignoring the criticism, they engaged with the reviewers and asked** for constructive feedback. They took this feedback on board to improve their writing for future books.

Key takeaway: Don't be defensive when faced with negative feedback. Use it as an opportunity to learn and grow.

The Travel Blogger: A travel blogger was experiencing burnout from constantly posting about their travels on social media. They took a break from posting for a few weeks and instead focused on engaging with their existing followers. They started asking for travel recommendations and sharing stories from their followers' travels. This helped them build a stronger community and renewed their passion for social media.

Key takeaway: Taking breaks and prioritizing engagement over constant content creation is important.

The Online Store: An online store struggled with low conversion rates from its social media ads. They started experimenting with different ad formats and targeting options until they found a winning combination that significantly increased sales.

Key takeaway: Don't be afraid to experiment and try new things until you find what works for your business.

The Non-Profit: A non-profit was having trouble getting donations on social media. They started sharing more personal stories from the people they helped, which helped to humanize their cause and inspire more gifts.

Key takeaway: Connect emotionally with your audience by sharing stories that resonate with them.

The Fitness Coach: **A** fitness coach had trouble getting engagement on their workout videos. They started sharing behind-the-scenes footage of their workouts and their struggles with fitness, which helped their followers connect with them on a more personal level.

Key takeaway: Authenticity and vulnerability can help build stronger connections with your audience.

Overall takeaway: Challenges on social media are inevitable, but with creativity, openness, and perseverance, businesses

and individuals can overcome them and
succeed.

Chapter 8: The Future of Social Media

Are you ready to gaze into the crystal ball and see what the future holds for social media? Are you prepared to witness the rise of the machines, the influencers' fall, and the memes' triumph? Well, buckle up because we're about to take a wild ride into the unknown territory of Chapter 8: The Future of social media!

As we approach the dawn of a new era, one thing is certain: social media is here to stay. It has revolutionized the way we communicate, connect, and consume information. But what does the future hold for this ever-evolving landscape? Will we be communicating via holograms? Will we have robots as social media managers? Or will we be living in a post-social media world? The possibilities are endless, and the future is exciting.

So, please put on your futuristic shades, grab your hoverboard, and delve into the unknown of what lies ahead for social media. Just don't forget to charge your phones because we don't want to miss out on any of the future's exciting social media developments!

Emerging trends and technologies in social media.

Social media is an ever-evolving world, and emerging trends and technologies continue to shape the way we interact with each other and consume information online. One such trend is the rise of video content, with live streaming and short-form video platforms like TikTok and Instagram Reels gaining popularity among users.

Additionally, augmented reality filters and virtual reality experiences are becoming more common on social media, offering new ways to engage with audiences.

Another emerging trend is using artificial intelligence and machine learning in social media, allowing for more personalized content and targeted advertising. Chatbots and virtual assistants are also becoming more prevalent, offering 24/7 customer service and support. Social commerce is also rising, with platforms like Instagram and Pinterest allowing users to shop directly from posts.

Privacy concerns and data protection remain major issues in the social media landscape. Users are becoming more aware of the information they share online and the potential for it to be used for targeted advertising or even nefarious purposes. This has led to the emergence of privacy-focused platforms like Telegram and Signal and increased scrutiny and regulation of social media companies.

As social media continues evolving, businesses and individuals must stay updated with the latest trends and technologies to remain relevant and competitive. This can involve experimenting with new platforms and features, engaging with audiences innovatively, and adapting to changing user behaviors and expectations.

To stay ahead of the curve, investing in ongoing education and training on social media best practices and emerging trends is important. Additionally, regularly monitoring and analyzing social media metrics can help identify areas for improvement and inform future strategies. By staying agile and adaptable, businesses and individuals can thrive in the ever-changing world of social media.

Key Takeaways:

1. Emerging trends in social media include video content, augmented reality, and the use of AI and machine learning.

2. Privacy concerns and data protection remain major issues in the social media landscape.

3. Social commerce is increasing, allowing users to shop directly from posts.

4. Staying current with the latest trends and technologies is important for staying relevant and competitive.

5. Ongoing education and training can help businesses and individuals stay ahead of the curve.

6. Regular monitoring and analysis of social media metrics can inform future strategies and identify areas for improvement.

How to stay up to date with the latest developments in social media

1. Follow industry experts and thought leaders on social media platforms and subscribe to their newsletters or blogs to stay informed about the latest trends and updates.

2. Join social media groups and communities to network with other

professionals in your field and exchange insights on the latest developments.

3. Attend industry conferences and events like Social Media Week or the Social Media Marketing World to learn from keynote speakers and network with other professionals.

4. Set up Google Alerts for industry keywords and topics to receive daily or weekly email updates on the latest news and developments in social media.

5. Monitor industry hashtags on social media platforms like #socialmedia or #digitalmarketing to stay informed about the latest conversations and trends.

6. Sign up for free online courses or webinars on social media topics to learn from industry experts and stay updated with the latest strategies and tools.

7. Use social media listening tools like Hootsuite or Mention to track industry conversations and stay informed about the latest news and trends.

8. Follow social media influencers and trendsetters on platforms such as Instagram, TikTok, or Twitter to stay informed about the latest trends in content creation and consumer behavior.

9. Read industry publications and blogs, such as Social Media Examiner, Buffer, or Hubspot, to stay informed about the

latest news and updates in the social media industry.

Remember to regularly review and adjust your social media strategies and tactics based on the latest developments and trends in the industry to ensure that you stay ahead of the competition.

Strategies for adapting to changes and staying relevant in the fast-paced world of social media.

1. **Stay current:** Keep track of the latest trends and changes in the social media landscape by following industry blogs, attending webinars and conferences, and subscribing to newsletters.

2. **Experiment with new features:** Don't be afraid to try out new features and tools social media platforms use. This can give you an edge over your

competitors and help you stay ahead of the curve.

3. **Engage with your audience:** Stay engaged by responding to comments, feedback, and messages. This will help you build a loyal following and maintain a positive reputation.

4. **Analyze your data:** Regularly analyze your social media data to identify patterns, trends, and areas for improvement. Use this information to refine your strategy and make data-driven decisions.

5. **Collaborate with others**: Collaborate with other businesses, influencers, or experts in your industry to tap into new audiences and reach new customers.

6. **Focus on quality over quantity:** Don't be too focused on the number of followers or likes you have. Instead, focus on creating high-quality content that resonates with your target audience.

7. **Use visuals:** Use engaging content, such as images and videos, to capture your audience's attention and make your brand more memorable.

8. **Embrace new platforms:** Watch for emerging social media platforms relevant to your audience or industry. Being an early adopter can give you an advantage in building a following.

9. **Test and iterate:** Try different approaches and tactics, and test what works best for your audience. Don't be

afraid to make changes and iterate on your strategy as you go.

10.   **Have fun:** social media is supposed to be fun, so don't take it too seriously. Embrace your brand's personality and have fun with your content to make a lasting impression on your audience.

Chapter 9: Conclusion

Ladies and gentlemen, boys, and girls, it's time for the grand finale of our social media journey. As we approach the end of this adventure, let's take a moment to reflect on all the things we've learned, the challenges we've faced, and the laughs we've shared. It's been an emotional rollercoaster, a wild ride filled with thrills and spills, and I think we can all agree that we've grown as individuals and as a community.

We've covered everything from identifying goals and audiences to creating killer content and building a loyal following. We've learned about the different platforms available and how to choose the right one for our needs. We've discussed the value of community and how to measure success and

ROI. And we've even peeked into the future to see what's in store for social media.

We've covered everything from identifying goals and audiences to creating killer content and building a loyal following. We've learned about the different platforms available and how to choose the right one for our needs. We've discussed the value of community and how to measure success and ROI. And we've even peeked into the future to see what's in store for social media.

It's been a wild ride, but all good things must come to an end. As we approach the final chapter of this epic saga, I invite you to sit back, relax, and enjoy the ride. It's been an honor to be your guide on this journey, and I hope you've enjoyed the ride as much as I have. So, without further ado, let's dive into the conclusion and wrap this baby up!

Recap of the key takeaways and lessons learned.

Throughout this book, we've covered a lot of ground in the exciting world of social media. From identifying goals and audiences to choosing the right platform, creating engaging content, building a community, and measuring success, we've explored the ins and outs of social media marketing.

Major Takeaways:

1. Set clear goals and objectives and understand your target audience before starting any social media marketing campaign.

2. Choose the right platform based on your goals and audience.

3. Create engaging content that aligns with your brand's personality and values.

4. Curate content from other sources to supplement your own.

5. Build a community by engaging with your audience, responding to comments and feedback, and promoting user-generated content.

6. Measure success by tracking your progress towards your goals and evaluating your ROI.

7. Stay updated with the latest trends and technologies in social media to adapt to changes and stay relevant.

Remember, social media is a dynamic and constantly evolving landscape, so staying agile and adaptable is important. By following these key takeaways, you'll be well on your way to creating a strong social media presence and driving meaningful engagement with your audience.

Final thoughts and advice for those starting social media.

- Congratulations, you made it to the end of this social media journey! Remember, social media is all about being social. Be yourself, have fun, and don't take yourself too seriously.

- Always remember that it's not about the number of followers but the quality of the relationships you build. And don't worry if your social media strategy doesn't work out at first. Just keep trying, keep learning, and keep evolving.

- Also, stay current on the latest social media trends and technologies. Who knows, maybe we'll all communicate through holographic emojis in a few years.

- But most importantly, never forget the golden rule of social media: treat others as you would like to be treated. Unless you're a masochist, who enjoys being bombarded with spammy messages and irrelevant content.

- And now, to leave you with one final social media joke: Why did the social media influencer break up with her boyfriend? Because he didn't like or comment on any of her posts.

- Encouragement to keep pushing forward and to never give up on social media success.

Postscript

Dear social media trailblazer,

As you journey through the world of social media, there will be times when the going gets tough, and it seems like the whole world is against you. But I urge you to keep pushing forward, for it is in the face of adversity that true success is forged.

Remember that social media success is not an overnight journey; it takes time, effort, and dedication. You may encounter setbacks and obstacles, but these are just bumps you can overcome with perseverance and resilience.

Celebrate your victories, no matter how small they may seem. Take the time to reflect on your progress and use it as fuel to keep moving forward. Keep experimenting, trying new things, and learning from your mistakes.

And most importantly, never forget why you started in the first place. Whether it's to connect with like-minded individuals, promote your brand, or have fun, always keep that passion burning in your heart.

So, my fellow social media adventurer, I leave you with this: keep pushing forward, keep striving for excellence, and never, ever give up. The world of social media is yours for the taking, and I can't wait to see what you will achieve.

www.ingramcontent.com/pod-product-compliance
Lightning Source LLC
Chambersburg PA
CBHW071137220526
45467CB00015B/1335